Your Driver Has Arrived

Ridesharing Stories by

Nestor "The Boss" Gomez

Your Driver Has Arrived

Ridesharing Stories by
Nestor "The Boss" Gomez

Tortoise Books
Chicago, IL

FIRST EDITION, AUGUST, 2020

©2020 Nestor Gomez

All rights reserved under International and Pan-American Copyright Convention

Published in the United States by Tortoise Books.

www.tortoisebooks.com

ASIN: XXX

ISBN-13: 978-1-948954-15-0

This book is a work of memoir, and is drawn from the author's experience, various artifacts and photographs, and recollections going back to an early age. Dialogue is approximate and appears in quotation marks for the benefit of the reader.

Cover design by Victor Calahan and Gerald Brennan

Tortoise Books Logo Copyright ©2020 by Tortoise Books. Original artwork by Rachele O'Hare.

When I first arrived to Chicago from Guatemala in the mid-80s

I was undocumented

I stuttered

And I didn't know the English language.

I didn't have a voice.

Today, I am a U.S. citizen

I am a storyteller

And I speak English (with a very sexy Latino accent)

I have found my "voz" (voice).

Therefore

I want to dedicate this book

To all my fellow immigrants

And to all those who feel as if they don't have a voice.

-     *Nestor "The Boss" Gomez*

It all started a couple of years ago. I was driving downtown on my way to a bookstore, when suddenly…

A car appeared in the street. That car was wearing a mustache.

"What was that?" I thought. "That thing in the front of the car?"

I couldn't believe what I had just seen, a car with a mustache. I needed to call my brother. He always seemed to know what was going on, or at least how to find out about it.

"HEY! You will not believe what I just saw…a car with a mustache…Yes, a car with a mustache. No, no, no, I don't mean a mustang. I mean a car with a mustache. *Bigote*, mustache…No, I don't know what it means, I thought you knew. You always seem to know about these things…Listen, I am on my way to the bookstore, you are in your office pretending to work. Why don't you get on your computer and see what you can find about cars with mustaches? Let me know later. OK?"

I went to the bookstore, and after a couple of hours reading, I forgot all about the car with the mustache.

A few months later I went to my mother's house to celebrate her birthday. My brother was there, but he was acting very strange. He kept checking his phone every other minute until suddenly after looking at his phone, he left in a hurry.

He came back a couple hours later.

"Hey, what's going on with you?" I asked. "It's Mom's birthday, but you left for a long time."

"I couldn't help it," he said. "I had to pick up a ride, and after I dropped that person, I got another ride request nearby."

"What are you talking about? Are you driving a taxi now?"

"Not a taxi," he explained. "I signed up with my phone and get ride requests through the application and get paid directly to my bank account at the end of the week. I get to use my own car, and they give me a cool mustache to put on the front."

"A mustache?"

"Yes," he said. "I got five hundred dollars just for signing up, then another five hundred dollars for recommending drivers. I got a couple of friends and my wife to sign up. I made over two thousand dollars in recommendations this month alone."

All I could think about was how I was the one who had told him about the mustache in the first place, and how I should have been the one making all that money.

"Do you want to sign up?" he asked me. "You get five hundred dollars if you complete twenty rides in the first week, and you get a mustache for your car."

I signed up to be a driver. Who could say no to a mustache for your car?

The first day that I drove, I realized I had no idea what I had signed up for.

The mustache I was given came with two small Velcro ties. Those were the only ties allowed to be used when attaching the mustache to the front of my car. But as soon as I started driving, I could see the mustache flipping over and laying on top of my hood, instead of being displayed on the front bumper.

I pulled over to the side and fixed the mustache several times before finally deciding to drive with the mustache flipped over and on top of the hood. But Chicago is the Windy City. I had been driving only a few minutes when suddenly the mustache got detached from my car. It flew over my car and landed on the other side of the road.

I had to pull over and get out of my car as fast as I could. I had to run across the street, and run some more trying to catch the mustache, which had been taken by the wind like some sort of renegade kite. Once I was able to capture the mustache, I got back in my car and decided to keep the mustache inside the car, leaning against the windshield. That made visibility difficult, and I also had to keep the mustache from sliding over to the passenger side.

I decided to call my brother and ask him for advice.

"Yeah," he responded when I mentioned the problems I was having. "You need to buy some extra thread and properly secure the mustache to your bumper. Otherwise it will fly all over the place."

"But the instructions clearly read that only the two ties provided are to be used," I reminded him.

"How is the working out?" he asked.

"Fine," I responded.

But I knew I would have to make some rules of my own if I wanted to be successful as a ridesharing driver.

"At least," I thought, "I will not have problems getting lost in the city."

I thought that way because I had lived in Chicago for over twenty years, and I thought I knew the city very well. But that was before I started driving. I realized there was so much I didn't know about the city.

For example, Lower Wacker Drive. I had always stayed away from it, because it seemed that if you didn't know you way around it, you could get lost down there very easily.

However, one of the very first passengers I drove was going to a hotel downtown, and the GPS told me to get on Lower Wacker Drive. At first, I figured that it would be OK. After all, the GPS was going to tell me which way to go. But as soon as I drove into Lower Wacker, the phone lost connection, the GPS went silent, and I was left to find the way out on my own. I took the first way out that I saw, and then after finding myself on ground level, I managed to find my way around the city. It was confusing, and my passenger was not pleased with my driving. I promised myself to stay away from Lower Wacker Drive.

A couple of weeks later I picked a passenger at Navy Pier, and the passenger told me to get in Lower Wacker to avoid the traffic downtown.

"I'd rather stay away from that area," I told the passenger. "The GPS doesn't work down there, and without it I might get lost."

"Don't worry," he replied. "I know my way around down there. I can guide you through, I will be your GPS."

He instructed me how to get there from Navy Pier, and he explained to me the way in and out of the first streets we came across as we drove into Lower Wacker.

"Did you know that this is where they filmed the Batman movie?" he asked as I drove.

I had seen the Batman movie about ten times, and I realized that he was right. No wonder the road had looked familiar to me, even though I had seldom driven down there. Suddenly I felt like I was the Dark Knight, on my way to rescue a damsel in distress. I even looked to my right at the small space where I could still see the Chicago River, to see if there was a Batman signal calling out to me in the sky.

"Yeah," the passenger said, interrupting my daydream. "They filmed a good chunk of the movie down here."

"Cool, that's something I can share with my future passengers," I said. But now I was feeling a bit less like Batman and a bit more like Robin, just driving Batman around.

With his help I got out of Lower Wacker with no problem, and then I continued driving until I reached his destination.

However, the very next day I received an e-mail from the ridesharing company. It turned out that my helpful passenger had complained about my lack of knowledge of the city. He had written about how concerned he was for his safety since I seemed "reckless" as I drove. He even complained about how difficult it was to understand me due to my "broken English."

The worst part of it was that his complaint had damaged my rating as a driver. Because of that, my earnings for that weekend were only a quarter of what I had expected, since getting a lower rating meant losing on the bonus money the company gave to drivers with high ratings.

A few days later, I was driving around when I got a request. I drove to pick up my fare, and when I got to the address a young man was on the sidewalk waiting for me.

I waited for him to get in the car, but instead he knocked on the window and told me he had ordered the ride for his mom, who needed to be driven to the Metra station on Randolph and Michigan. He told me that she needed to get there by 6:00 p.m. It was almost 5:45 already.

Now, it is possible to get from Bucktown (or like I always call it, "Hipster Town") to Randolph and Michigan in fifteen minutes, or even in ten minutes, but not in a Wednesday afternoon in the middle of rush hour.

I explained this to the young man and told him that I would have to cancel the ride because there was no way I could get to the destination in fifteen minutes. The young man gave me a desperate look, and I was familiar with that look. It's the look one makes when your mother is driving you crazy.

I agreed to drive his mother to the train station, but I told him that it would probably take me more than fifteen minutes to get there.

"It doesn't matter, just take her away," he said. "Mom will just have to take the next train. Just don't tell her she is going to be late, or she will be upset."

"If you don't tell her, I won't tell her!" I responded. He went back into his house and came back out holding the arm of a very grumpy-looking old lady. The lady was complaining about how steep the steps were, and how offended she was that she was being rushed. The young man helped his mother into my car, and with a huge smile on his face, he waved her goodbye.

I couldn't understand how he could be smiling when the lady was so mean to him.

"You know where you are going?" the old lady asked me. But before I could answer, she added: "Put the address in the GPS thing, so you don't get lost."

I put the address in the GPS, and the GPS lady said "You will arrive at your destination by 6:20 p.m."

"6:20 p.m.," the old lady said. "You people are always making me late."

I got mad. Mad at the GPS lady for telling us that we were going to be late, and mad at the old lady for saying "You people." Now, I don't know if she said it because I am Latino, because I'm a person of color, or because I was a ridesharing driver. But I decided right then and there that I was going to get the old lady to her destination by 6:00 p.m. I would show her that "my people" can do a really good job. Even if I didn't know who "my people" were in her mind.

I started driving, and both the old lady and the GPS lady told me to take the expressway.

I ignored them both and drove past the expressway.

Immediately, the old lady and the GPS lady told me to make a U-turn and head back to the expressway.

"Listen, both of you!" I said. "It's rush hour right now. If I get on there, we'll never make it on time. I'm taking another route."

"Fine," the old lady answered. "But you better get me there on time."

"Rerouting," the GPS lady said.

So I drove on a street that runs next to the expressway. I drove as fast as I could without the old lady complaining I was going too fast. When the street came to an end I took a side street, and then another, and then an alley. Meanwhile the

GPS lady kept saying "Make a left. Rerouting. Make a right. Rerouting." And the old lady kept complaining that I was lost.

Finally I was getting close to Randolph, but I needed to head east, and Randolph is a one-way street going west, so I made a left on Lake. This was a gamble because Lake is usually packed with cars, but somehow today it was almost empty. I made it all the way to Michigan Avenue with five minutes to spare.

Or so I thought.

I turned right onto Michigan. We were only one block away from the destination with a few cars ahead of us but the traffic light was red. Four minutes left, three minutes left, and the light finally changed. The cars ahead barely moved, and we got stuck at the light again. Two minutes left, one minute left, and the light changed again. I drove through the intersection and parked in front of the station as the clock changed to 6:00.

"We made it!" I said.

"What do you mean, 'We made it,'" the old lady said. "I still have to get to my train. You people are always making me late."

I didn't say anything. The GPS lady didn't say anything, either. I guess she was as surprised and hurt as I was.

One of the best things about driving people around is that I got to know the city very well. I thought I had known it before, but I came to understand Lower Wacker Drive. And the Upper and Lower Michigan and Illinois Streets. And the expressways. And Logan, Palmer, and Lincoln Square. The North, South, and West Side. This wonderful city of ours.

Not all the rides were bad as the one with the two crazy ladies. But some were worse.

On one occasion I got a request from a guy who happened to be standing across the street from where I had parked my car to wait. I made a U-turn in order to get to the other side of the street and pick him up, but I overcompensated, and my car went over the sidewalk a little. OK, a lot.

After a few bumps and jumps I parked the car to let the man get in. He got into my car and started to reprimand me for making a U-turn. He complained that I was driving unsafely, and said I should turn the radio off in order to pay more attention to the road. I turned it off just in time to hear him ask me where I was from.

"Are you Mexican?" he asked, as if that immediately meant I was a bad driver.

"Actually, I am from Guatemala" I replied. "My first wife was Mexican," I added, trying to have a friendly conversation.

"So did you have a lot of kids?" he asked. "Those Mexicans sure have lots of kids."

"Well, Mexico is a very Catholic country, and the religion forbids contraception and abortion. But no, we only had two kids," I said. I was trying not to sound pissed off. "But don't worry," I added. "I divorced the Mexican and married someone else."

"Oh," he said. "Where was your second wife from?"

"She was Mexican," I replied.

"No kids?" he asked.

"No kids. She wanted a kid, but I had already decided two were enough. That eventually drove us apart, and we got a divorce."

"Good for you," he said, all sure of himself. "Those Mexicans are all drug dealers and rapists that come to this country to live off welfare."

I had told this man that my two ex-wives were Mexicans, and that my kids were obviously half-Mexican. You would think that he would be smart enough to deduce that I had friends who are Mexicans, and that I wouldn't let him insult Mexicans just because I wasn't one of them.

I told him that I know many people who are from Mexico, and that the great majority are hardworking people who have come to this country to provide a better life for their loved ones, and that the only crime they might have committed was crossing the border undocumented.

"But you are Guatemalan," he said. "Your people are different."

"How so?"

"Your people came here as refugees from the civil war in your country," he responded.

"Actually," I said, "I crossed the Mexican border undocumented. And then I crossed the USA

border also undocumented, so that makes me
twice as bad as the Mexicans."

He started to tell me how people are disrespecting
the flag of the South, and how minorities are taking
over the country. He tried to tell me that I should
have applied for a visa instead of crossing the
border, and he would not listen as I tried to
explain that some of my family members living in
Guatemala were still waiting for a visa more than
twenty years after applying for one. "That's why
some people can't wait for a visa and come to this
country undocumented," I said.

"We are going to put an end to that," he replied.
"We are going to make American great again by
building a wall to keep all the undocumented
people out."

Now there was nothing I could say; his comments
had already built a wall between us. I wanted to
pull the car over, reach back where he was seating,
and punch him on the face. But I knew that if I did
that, I could lose my job driving for the ridesharing
company, get in trouble with the police, or maybe
even lose the fight and get beat up. But most
importantly, by getting into a fight with him I

would be only giving him more reasons to dislike immigrants.

I just kept driving, trying to get him to his destination as fast as possible. When we arrived, he paused before leaving the car to tell me that he was not a racist, and that he only wanted to make America great again.

I drove away and parked a few blocks away, trying to calm down. I was so upset that I was actually shaking. I felt that I should just call it a night and go home. After all, that man had just ruined my whole night, and I was so upset that I would probably be rude to whoever my next passenger was. I was about to turn off the phone when I got another request. Since canceling a request would lower my rating, and with that, lower my pay, I decided to pick up the next passenger and then go home. I drove to pick up the request and saw three white guys waiting for me.

"Now there's three of them," I thought. But then I realized that I could not let myself behave that way. I couldn't judge a whole group of people based on the actions of one individual. So I checked myself, and pulled my car over to pick them up.

The three white guys got in my car, and I asked them if it was ok for me to listen to NPR while I drove. They said they loved NPR.

"Thank God," I said. "My last ride didn't care for NPR. He only wanted to make America great again."

They asked me what happened, and I started to recount my conversation with the previous ride. When I got to the part where I told him that I was twice undocumented, we were all laughing aloud.

In the end I was able to realize that although there are some haters out there, for each of them there are three, or maybe even ten, or maybe even more open-minded people that are trying to make not only America, but the whole world, a better place.

After a few months of driving for one ridesharing company, I signed up to drive for their competitor as well. Not only did I earn another five-hundred-dollar bonus by signing up for a second company, but it also gave me the opportunity to work more hours, and to change from one company to the other whenever one offered more money than the other. I worked through the holidays. I even decorated my car with Christmas lights and played Christmas songs on my radio. For New Year's I carried noisemakers and hats to celebrate, and of course for St. Valentine's I had roses for the ladies.

The weekend of St. Patrick's Day, my girlfriend asked me if I had decorated the car for that as well.

"Of course," I told her.

However, the only decorations I had put in my car were plastic covers on the seats to keep people from puking all over.

You might have deduced by now that I am not Irish. Also I don't like to drive drunk people around. That's why I wasn't excited about St. Patrick's Day.

I started driving Friday night, and the first passenger I picked up was drunk. He almost threw up in my car. The second passenger threw up right before getting in my car. The third one puked right after I drove him to his destination. The next one looked so drunk that I did not stop to pick him up. I canceled the request and kept driving home, without worrying if it was going to damage my rating. I decided to get up early the next morning instead of trying to avoid drunk people all night.

Saturday morning, I decided to take drastic measures in order to make up for lost money and time. I decided to embrace the spirit of the festivities. So I decorated not only my car, but also myself. I wore green pants and a green shirt. Green socks and shoes. I also wore a huge green hat. I even went through the trouble of buying a bunch of chocolate gold coins, which I placed inside a bucket to make them look like a pot of gold. I planned to give them to the riders as they got inside the car.

I got my first request and I drove to the pick-up destination. When I got there, it was a group of college girls. I got out of the car and opened the door for them. I held some chocolate coins in my hand, and using my best fake Irish accent, I asked them: "Would you like some of me gold?"

"Oh my God!" they answered. "We've never seen a Mexican leprechaun!"

Usually a comment like that would piss me off, but I found it very difficult to be upset at a group of beautiful girls just wanting to have fun. Especially because they wanted to take pictures with me. So I took some pictures with them. I figured: "The costumer is always right."

It seemed that maybe all that green I was wearing was going to bring me good luck. And it did. I was busy the whole morning, giving rides back and forth, nonstop.

Around 1:00 p.m. I got a request to pick someone up at Michigan and Randolph. I started driving without realizing that I was driving in the direction of the St. Patrick's Day parade.

As I got closer, it became obvious that picking up my fare was not going to be easy. But somehow I found myself near Michigan and Randolph. I stopped the car and texted the passenger: "Where are you?"

"At Michigan and Randolph," came back the reply.

There were hundreds of people at Michigan and Randolph. "What are you wearing?" I texted back.

"A green hat," came back the reply.

Everyone was wearing a green hat. Even I was wearing a green hat.

Just then I saw the person who had requested the ride waving at me from Michigan Ave. I saw a space opening in between the crowd, and without thinking I turned onto Michigan.

The person who requested the ride got in the passenger seat of my car right about the same time that two police officers turned to look in my direction. I suddenly realized that I had made an illegal turn, and that my car was now right at the end of the parade. The officers started to walk in my direction.

I turned to face the passenger. I took a bunch of chocolate coins from my pot of gold and put them in the passenger's hands.

"What am I supposed to do with all this chocolate?" the passenger asked.

"Throw it to the crowd!" I told him. I lowered the car's windows and took another bunch of coins, and we both started to throw the chocolate coins into the crowd.

The police officers looked at me and my huge green hat, green outfit, and gold coins. Then they looked at one another as if asking each other if I was part of the parade or not. I threw some coins at them. They caught the coins and smiled. And I kept on driving.

That was not the last time I had to deal with the police, though.

Driving a passenger to the airport was usually something I did not like to do. Although it promised a long and well-paid trip on the way there, it did not always mean that I would have a rider back into the city. Sometimes I would pick up a rider near the airport that would want to be taken farther away from the city, into one of the near suburbs. Then I might have another rider, and another. Eventually I would have to turn the application off and drive back to the city without a passenger. I would not be making any money on my drive back, and would be wasting both time and gas.

One day as I drove near the lakefront, I got a request to drive a group to the airport.

"We are on our first trip out of the country," they told me excitedly as they got in.

"Are you in a hurry to get there?" I asked. I wanted to make sure I wouldn't have to rush to get them to their flight on time.

"We are actually early," they responded.

I drove them to the airport, but I failed to take the exit to the departure area, and ended up at the arrival area instead.

I apologized for my mistake, and I offered to drive them back around the airport to the right spot.

"Let me turn of the application," I said, "to make sure you don't get charged extra for my mistake."

"You don't have to do that!" they assured me. "Just don't miss the exit again."

Still, I turned off the application.

As I started to drive away from the terminal, I noticed a police car behind me. It turned on its lights and pulled me over.

"Why did you pick these passengers?" the police officer asked when he got to my window.

"Because they wanted to go to the airport," I replied, confused.

"Did you picked them up at the terminal?" the officer asked.

"No, I picked them up by the lake," I replied. "I'm taking them to the departure area."

"Don't lie to me," the officer said. "I saw you driving away from the terminal."

One of my passengers tried to explain it to the police officer. "Officer, he picked us up by the lake, but he missed the exit."

"I didn't ask you," he replied angrily, without even looking at the passenger. "Let me see your phone," he said to me. When he saw my phone was no longer recording the trip, he said: "Did you turn off the application when I pulled you over?"

"I turned it off because I didn't want them to pay extra for my mistake," I explained.

"If you're lying to me, you are going to be in big trouble," the officer said. "You better tell me the truth."

"I'm not lying," I said.

"Let me see your phone," the officer said to the passenger that had spoken to him.

Luckily for me the passenger had not logged out of the application, and the trip was still showing on his phone.

"I see, you missed your exit," the officer said.

"That's why I was driving around the airport," I responded. "I didn't know it was a crime."

"The crime is picking up fares at the airport. Don't you know that?"

"Not at all," I replied. Apparently there was a new regulation that had been put in place after the taxi companies had complained about the ridesharing companies taking over the rides from the airport. I had not been aware of it.

I had been lucky to miss my exit and get pulled over when I did. Otherwise I would have tried to pick someone after dropping my fare, and I would have *really* gotten in trouble. At the time, ridesharing drivers that broke the rule were given a heavy fine, and their cars were impounded.

Instead, once I was able to drop my passengers to the right terminal, I kept the application off and drove back to the city, intending to stay away from the airport and the police as much as possible.

But only a few weeks later, I was again seeing the flashing lights.

It happened late one night as I was waiting for the light to make a left turn at an intersection. I heard the notification letting me know that I had just gotten a ride request. I looked over at my phone and saw that the pick-up location was only a few blocks ahead.

Without thinking it over, I decided not to make the left turn. Instead I pressed the gas and drove straight ahead. However, I failed to realize that there was a police car on the other side of the street, facing me, about to make a left turn. As I started to drive straight, the police car turned left into my path. Lucky for me he turned slowly, and swerved out of my way as I drove past the intersection.

Still, I knew I was in trouble.

I glanced in my rearview mirror just in time to see the police car's lights go on.

I didn't even wait for them to catch up to me, I just pulled over.

"What the fuck is wrong with you?" the policer officer screamed as he came over to my window.

"I'm sorry, officer," I replied.

Beep! Beep! Beep! My phone kept letting me know my passenger was nearby.

"Of course. You're too busy trying to pick up a passenger to drive safely," the officer said, looking at my phone. "Turn that shit off," he ordered.

"I'm sorry, officer," I said again. I turned my phone off.

"Give me your license and your insurance," he barked. As I handled him the documents, he said, "You better pray I don't find anything on your record."

"I'm sorry, sir," I said once again.

After a few minutes he came back to my window. "Your record is clean," he said. "But I'm still going to give you as many tickets as I can. You almost killed me back there. What the fuck is wrong with you?"

"I'm sorry, officer," I replied.

"Stop apologizing," he said. "That's not going to help you. Were you aware that…"

Before he could finish his sentence, his radio transmitter went off. There was some sort of emergency nearby.

The officer looked at me, handling me back my documents. "Get out of my face," he said.

Seconds later, the patrol car sped away.

I turned my phone back on. The person that had requested the ride had already canceled the request.

"I need to be more careful," I told myself. "I know better than to drive that way."

I drove away thankful that I had not ruined my car, my life, and probably somebody else's life in my urge to get to my destination.

I thought about going home, but a few minutes later I had received a new request, and I was on my way to pick them up. I made sure to drive safely, at a normal speed and following all the street signs, without making any last-minute maneuvers or illegal U-turns.

I picked up my passengers and started driving away, but only a few minutes into my drive, again I saw the police car lights.

"Why are they pulling you over?" one of my passengers asked.

"You haven't done anything wrong," the other one added.

I knew they were partially right. As far as the current ride was concerned, I had been driving properly.

But I couldn't help thinking that I was being pulled over by the same officer that had pulled me over just minutes before. Maybe the emergency that had sent him away had turned out to be a false alarm, and I was going to get all those tickets after all.

"Do you know why I pulled you over?" the officer asked.

I could see that this was not the officer that had pulled me over before. "Actually, no, I don't," I responded.

It turned out that my license plates had expired weeks before. I had not even realized it.

"Can you just let him go, without a ticket?" my passengers asked the officer. But he kept writing.

I thanked them for their concern, and then asked the officer if I could still take them to their destination.

"If any other officer pulls you over, just show them this ticket." He handed it to me. "And make sure to buy a new sticker for your plates," he added, before walking away.

After dropping my fare at their destination. I turned off the application and drove to a twenty-four-hour currency exchange. I bought the sticker for my plates, and a money order to pay the ticket I had been given.

Then I drove home. Despite the financial loss, I had been lucky. I did not want to tempt my luck any longer.

You never know what the rides have in store for you. Things happen so suddenly that you unsuspectedly become part of your riders' lives. Sometimes, you might be able to look the other way when a couple is kissing or arguing in the back, but it is more difficult to remain impartial when they ask your opinion. Especially when their opinions are in strong contrast to yours.

I drove to Lakeview to pick up a fare. I stopped in front of what looked like a million-dollar house. Three young white guys got out and started to walk towards the car. Now these white guys were wearing baseball caps, basketball t-shirts, and pants that showed their underwear. Wearing those clothes, coming out of a very fancy house, it looked like they were going to some costume party. And it wasn't anywhere near Halloween.

They got in my car. One guy sat next to me in the passenger seat, and the other two sat in the back.

Before I had a chance to ask for their destination, the man at the front reached over to my radio and changed the station. Instinctively, I looked at him in a way that said: Dude, don't touch my radio.

Now, I know that I am supposed to accommodate the passenger's requests, but this guy didn't even request anything. He just helped himself to my radio. And the golden rule is: Do not mess with the driver's radio. I was giving this guy "the look," but he seemed unable to understand it. But I had a five-star rating that I didn't want to mess up, so I decided to cool off. Maybe he didn't know any better.

Instead of giving him an attitude, I gave him a cord. That way he could hook up his phone and play whatever music he wanted. But as I started to drive, they began to play gangster rap music. Now, I don't have anything against any kind of music, and I strongly believe that anyone can listen to any kind of music that they want. But by the second song these guys were rapping along with it. I know that some white people can rap: Eminem, Vanilla Ice...OK, that's about it. But these guys sounded like drunk, clueless, tone-deaf Vanilla Ices.

I rolled my eyes and kept repeating to myself: "They don't know any better. They don't know any better."

A few songs later I looked in the rear-view mirror. Each of them had turned their caps in a different direction. One had his cap to the left, the other to the right, and the one at the front was wearing his backwards.

I thought to myself: "If these guys were really street, they would be killing each other right now. Each of them are wearing their caps in a way that identifies them as members of rival gangs."

But then I kept telling myself: "You need your five-star rating. They don't know any better."

Another song started playing, and all three of them lowered the windows and started to throw out signs. I stopped at a red light and again gave them my crazy look. But again, they didn't seem to know what I meant.

"Stop that!" I finally told them. "You can't be throwing signs out the window! Are you crazy?"

"Is this a dangerous hood?" one of them asked.

"Are we going to get shot?" another asked.

The third guy didn't say anything, he just ducked low in the chair, probably just in case, so he wouldn't get shot.

"No, it is not a dangerous hood," I told them, still giving them the crazy look. "We are driving by

Bucktown, there's nothing but hipsters up in here." But what I really wanted to say was: Yes, you will get shot, not because this is a dangerous hood, but because you look stupid throwing peace signs and OK signs out of the window of a car playing loud gangster music! Are you crazy?

Since I was still worried about my rating, I just told them I had to keep the windows up because the AC was on. Then I raised and locked all the windows.

I was only a couple of blocks away from their destination when a song that is famous for having a large number of N-words on it started to play. The guys got really excited. They started to act more street than ever. When the song got to the first N-word, I clearly heard the *BEEP* from the radio. But the three guys said the N-word, and repeated it over and over and over.

I pulled the car over and gave them my craziest look ever. This time they understood.

"We were just singing alone, bro," one of the guys said.

"I picked you up at Lakeview, and I am driving you to Wicker Park. There's nothing but yuppies up in here, and there's nothing street about you guys," I told them angrily. "But even if you had some street creed, even if you were going to Englewood or Humboldt Park or at least Hyde Park, even then, you don't get to say the N-word! I am Latino, a person of color, and I don't get to say the N-word! Only black people can say the N-word."

"Dude, you are not even black. Why are you so upset?" another guy asked.

"I am not black," I said. "But I am a Latino. A person of color. Our struggles are entwined."

"Well, you are going to be struggling, because I am going to complain about you and rate you a one-star," the third guy said.

And I gave them a look. A look that said two things:

One: I don't care a *BEEP* about ratings or stars right now.

And two: You need to get the *BEEP* out of my car right now.

This time they seemed to finally understand my angry look. They got out of the car, without saying another word.

I drove the next couple of blocks with my right fist raised high in the air.

I was still working my regular morning job, in addition to my afternoons and weekends driving for two ride-sharing companies. Maybe I was working too many hours and not getting enough sleep, because I started to lose my patience with some of my riders.

I picked up a trio of guys on their way to a bar. They all sat in the back of the car and started to make jokes among themselves.

I started driving without paying too much attention to their conversation. Suddenly at a red light, I noticed that one of them had lowered one of the back windows and was now whistling to a woman walking on the sidewalk.

I closed the window without saying a word.

As I restarted driving, I heard the window going down again. This time, the trio of guys were catcalling a young lady walking by.

"Hey, hey, hey, what's your name?" screamed one of them.

"Forget your name, give me your number, girl!" screamed another.

The third guy asked for a lot more than her name or number. They all started laughing and high-fiving one another.

"Would you mind keeping the window closed?" I asked them as I closed the windows from my driver seat.

"Why?" one of the guys asked.

"Well," I responded, "the air conditioner is on, and the windows must remain closed."

A couple of blocks later, the trio again lowered one of the windows and started harassing a female walking down the street.

Again, I closed the window, but this time I made sure to lock the windows to keep them from lowering them again.

That didn't keep the trio from harassing another female a few minutes later. This time they were tapping on the window and making obscene gestures.

"Do you honestly think women enjoy your catcalling?" I asked them, looking at them through my rearview mirror.

"Of course they do," they responded. "They love it!"

"I used to think that," I told them. "In fact, as a teenager I used to hide outside my house waiting for my mother coming back from work, and I would run and snatch her purse to scare her. I thought it was funny, I never stopped to think that I could have been seen by a police officer and gotten in trouble before I could explain myself. Or that my mother walking alone at night might have gotten scared and had a heart attack. Or mad, and killed me once we got home."

"That's different," one of them argued. "What you did was a stupid game you played with your mom. What we do is to praise women for looking hot."

"But my immature game and nature stayed with me as I became a young adult," I continued. "By then, I would hide whenever I saw one of my female friends walking alone in the street. And then from my hiding place, I would start catcalling them. 'Hey baby, what's your name!' Then when I noticed that they had started to feel uneasy, I would come out of my hiding space. 'It's just me,' I would say, smiling. 'I bet you thought it was some creepy guy messing with you.' I was too ignorant to realize that my prank turned me into the creepy guy.

"And it only got worse," I continued. "One time, I was at a party with my girlfriend, when I lost my phone. A few days later my girlfriend went to her sister's house, to babysit her niece. That same day I happened to find my phone. A friend of mine had taken it by mistake and then had returned it to me. But I didn't call my girlfriend to tell her I had my phone. Instead I thought it would be funny if I used my phone to trick her. 'Hey baby,' I texted her from my phone. 'Who is this?' she texted back, not knowing I had my phone back. 'Who are you?' I texted back. 'Are you alone?'

"And then I continued to text, pretending to be some stranger than had found the phone and was trying to contact her. While I was laughing at my stupid prank, my girlfriend was getting more and more worried by the minute. She thought that some stranger has found my phone and was now stalking her, while she was alone with a two-year-old at her sister's house. Which had been broken into just a few days prior."

"The following day, when she found out it had been me texting her, she got really mad. 'I was just playing with you,' I told her. 'Do you have any idea how worried I was that someone was trying to come to my sister's house and hurt me and my niece?' she said. 'Do you have any idea how dangerous your stupid prank was?'

"I apologized. I was lucky she didn't break up with me that day," I explained to the guys. "In fact, we are still together, and I have been trying to be a better person than I used to be. Like the other day, I got home late from driving. 'Is that you?' she asked when I got in the house. 'Yeah,' I said. 'I'm so glad you're home,' she said. 'Did you miss me?' I asked, getting ready to jump into bed. She said, 'Yeah. And the dogs need to go out.'

"At first, I was mad at her. But then I realized that it was safer for me to take the dogs out than to have her do it. After all, as a man there are a lot less possibilities that I get attacked, robbed, or harassed at that hour than there is for my girlfriend." I looked back at them, hoping they had learned a lesson.

"Wait," one of the guys asked. "You have a girlfriend?"

"Sure," I said.

"We thought you were gay," another one of them said.

"You heard the story I just told you, and all you got from it was that you thought I was gay?" I was annoyed.

"Dude, you were acting so weird! Just because we were messing with some girls!"

"I just tried to tell you why," I answered. "I don't think you should be making those kind of remarks. I…"

"Dude, we are here," one of the guys said, pointing across the street to the bar which was their destination. They started to exit my vehicle before I could finish my comment.

I felt annoyed as they crossed the street and disappeared from my view. Not at the fact that they had thought I was gay. I am old enough, and hopefully mature enough, to be secure with my masculinity. No, I was annoyed that they thought it was necessary for them to harass women in order to feel secure in their masculinity. I drove away hoping it wouldn't take them as long as it took me to learn and act better.

Late one night I was parked near the corner of Lake and Racine waiting for a pick-up request, when suddenly I saw a young lady walking down the street.

That part of town is kind of dark and isolated. Not the best part of town to be taking a walk, especially at two in the morning. Anyway, the young lady was going west on Lake, and as she walked she kept looking behind her. Then suddenly she took off running. Instead of heading south toward the busier and illuminated streets like Randolph and Washington, she was running north, towards Grand and the train tracks. I didn't see anybody following her.

My first instinct was to mind my own business and just drive away. But then I realized that once she reached the train tracks, she would be almost on a dead-end street. What if someone was indeed following her? At this hour, no one would hear her scream for help.

I drove my car in the direction I had last seen her run. When I turned my car down the side street, I could see her at a distance, running full-speed. I slowed down and hit the beam lights so the street could be properly illuminated. The girl stopped running and started to look up and down the street like she was looking for her car. I stopped my car about half a block away and continued illuminating the dark street. I didn't want to get any closer. I didn't want her to think I was some sort of pervert.

Suddenly she started to walk towards me. As she approached my car, she reached for the passenger door. I lowered my window and asked if she was OK.

"I'm trying to get to my car," she said. "I just can't remember where I parked."

She told me name of the street where she had left the car. I told her that it was a few blocks north and a couple of blocks east. She looked at me like

I was talking to her in a foreign language. "Can you just give me a ride to my car?" she asked.

"Only if you text the plate number of my car to one of your friends," I responded.

She asked why, and I told her that she should always do that before getting into a stranger's car. "But you drive people for a living," she said, pointing at the ride-sharing emblems in my windshield.

I had to explain to her that she had not requested a ride using the application, and therefore she had none of my information. "I am not supposed to do this," I told her, "but I am going to do you a favor and drive you to your car, just because this is not a very safe part of town."

Once she got in my car, she told me how she had been at a nearby bar, and some guy had offered to buy her a drink. She had declined, but the guy had kept bugging her. She had felt uncomfortable, and had decided to leave, but once she did she saw the guy walking out as well. She had started to walk faster, and had felt the guy following her. That's when she had started running. But she was so nervous that she had forgotten how to get back to her car.

"You should be more careful," I said.

"I know," she responded.

"Is this where you parked?" I asked, as we pulled up to the location she had told me.

She pointed to her car. As she was about to leave, she tried to put some money in my hands.

I refused the money. I told her I had a son and a daughter about her age, and I hoped that if one day my kids needed help, they could find someone to help them.

I saw the young lady drive away. I prayed to God that she made it home safe, and I prayed to God to keep everyone else's daughter safe, too.

By this time, I had been driving for the ridesharing companies for almost a year.

I made my way late one night to pick up a passenger. There was a group of about six guys at the exit of a bar. I wondered if my passenger was amongst them.

"I hope he doesn't try to bring the whole group in my car," I told myself. "This ain't no clown car."

My mind drifted back to my first day as a ridesharing driver. I was given a training session by an experienced driver. He told me how to use the application, and to be aware that I will be rated by my passengers on my driver performance. He also warmed me to never let too many people ride in my car. "You can get pulled over and get a ticket," he had said. "Let them know they all have to have their seat belts on."

But as a driver, I quickly learned that some people didn't care about safety. Especially drunk people. I had to refuse to start the car until they let some people out, or until they canceled the ride and ordered a bigger vehicle.

Suddenly I heard someone knocking on my car window. It was my passenger. He was alone, but he was obviously very drunk. He sat in the back seat, and as soon as he sat, he made a noise as if he was about to puke.

"If someone pukes in your car," the instructor had told me, "make sure to take a picture of them and the damage, so you can charge them the three-hundred-dollar cleaning fee."

I got my phone ready just in case I had to take a picture. But at the last minute, the passenger opened the door and puked on the sidewalk.

The application told me where my passenger was going, but I asked him, just to be sure.

"Always, always, double-check their destination address," my instructor had told me. "Especially if they are drunk. You don't want to drive them to the wrong place, and then have them blame you for it."

"Ah ha, ah ha," my passenger said as an affirmation. I started driving. Soon I heard him snoring in the back seat.

"If your passenger ever falls sleep," my instructor had told me, "don't take them for a longer ride than they need. They can always check the route you took in their application the next day."

"And how do I wake them up?" I had asked. "Can I shake them, or poke them?"

"Only if you want to be sued," he had answered. "You just have to talk to them and give them a few minutes to wake up."

But I had been driving for a while now, and I knew that talking never woke the drunk, sleeping passengers. So as I got my drunk passenger to his destination, I parked the car, turned my radio on, and raised the volume all the way up. The passenger sat up and looked around a bit, confused.

"We are here," I said. I thought that if my instructor could see me now, he would be so proud of me.

Just then, my passenger got out of my car into the cold winter air. He took a few drunken steps and fell face-first into a bank of snow on the sidewalk.

My first instinct was to drive away.

"You are not supposed to touch them," I heard myself thinking as I got out of my car to help the guy. Against my better judgment, I grabbed him by his coat and helped him up. He leaned against my body to keep from falling.

"That thing you did with the radio to wake me up," he said. "That was a nice trick."

"What are you talking about?" I asked.

"I didn't teach you that," he said, with a drunk smile.

I looked at him in shock.

"Don't you recognize me?" he asked. "I'm your instructor."

It was true.

"I got to tell you," he added. "You have come a long way."

"Thanks," I said. "But let's worry about you now. Can you make it all the way to your house?"

He shook his head no. So I helped him get to his door. I stood there as he tried in vain to use his keys. Finally, I took the keys from him and opened the door myself. The door opened to a flight of stairs.

"I live on the second floor," he said. "But I don't think I can make the stairs on my own."

He leaned heavily on me as I helped him up the stairs. This time he didn't even try to open the door, he just looked at me. So I opened the door, put the keys in his coat pocket, and pushed him inside the apartment. Maybe I pushed him a little bit too hard, because he fell face-first in the middle of the living room.

I closed the door and ran back to my car.

The next day, I checked my phone to see how much money I had made driving the night before. There was an email. It was from my instructor.

My instructor was praising me as a driver. He didn't mention the fact that he had been drunk and fallen in the snow, but he praised me as a driver, and ended by stating that the student had surpassed the teacher.

And I told myself, "You are right about that."

I had driven for a couple of hours.

It was a slow night with not many requests. By this time, there were a lot more ridesharing drivers on the road, and the increased competition had started to hurt my profit margin. That night, I had waited a long time in between requests, and I had decided to stop driving early and head home.

I stopped at a red light, and a guy came up and knocked on my door.

"Where are you heading?" he asked as soon as I lowered my window.

"Home," I replied.

"Are you heading north?" he asked.

"What difference does it make?" I responded. I did not want to give him any clue of where I lived.

"Give us a ride," he said pointing to a girl standing next to him.

"You have to request a ride using the application," I answered, pointing to my phone.

"If you're heading that way, we don't have to use the application," he responded. "You can make some cash, and we get to save some money."

I knew that I was taking a chance by giving them a ride without them using the application. In case of an accident, the ridesharing insurance would not cover me. And they also looked drunk enough to puke in my car, and I knew I would not be able to collect a cleaning fee.

"Where exactly are you heading to?" I asked.

The guy opened the door to my car and guided the woman inside and gave me the address. It was only a few blocks away from my house.

Since I was heading home for the night, I decided I would take my chances and drive them. "I can always use a few bucks for gas," I told myself.

Just in case, I kept one eye on the road and one eye on the rearview. The more I drove, the more I realized what a dangerous position I had put myself into. When I drove someone using the app, I had some information about them. However, this time I was on my own, with two complete strangers in the back of my car.

I was relieved when I got to their destination without incident.

The woman got out of my car and started to walk away as the guy stayed in the back seat searching in his pants for some cash.

"Oh, dude," he said after a few minutes fumbling in his pockets. "I don't have any cash." He showed me his empty hands and proceeded to get out.

I lowered my window to scream at him. "Hey, what the hell!"

"Dude," he responded, "thanks for the ride." And he continued to walk away.

I sat in my car for a second, unsure of what to do. I wanted to get out and confront him. But I knew that if I went out and started an argument and someone called the police, he was going to deny me giving him a ride. Or I was going to get in trouble for giving him a ride without using the application, which was against the ridesharing rules.

"At least they didn't puke in the car," I told myself.

But then I realized that I hadn't looked in the back of the car yet.

I looked back, dreading the worst. The back seats looked clean, but from where I was seating, I couldn't see the floor. I undid my seat belt, got out of my car and opened the back door, and that's when I saw it.

They had left a phone in my car. And it wasn't just any phone, it was the latest model, worth hundreds of dollars.

I looked down the street and I could still see the guy walking a few steps behind his date. I took the phone in my hand, got back in my car and started driving his way.

"Dude, just drive away," he said as I drove up.

"Fine," I said. "I will just keep this phone as payment for the ride." I let him see the phone as I started to drive away. But before the end of the block I stopped, got out, and started to walk towards him.

"Hey, give me back my phone!" he screamed.

"If you won't pay me for the ride, at least pay me for returning your phone," I said.

"All I got is a twenty," he said, and took a bill out of his pocket.

I snatched the bill out of his hand and threw the phone on the ground next to him.

He started complaining that I had damaged his phone, but I ignored him and drove away. I promised myself to never again pick up anyone without using the application.

The crowd was counting down the seconds left till midnight. 3…2…1…HAPPY NEW YEAR!

I turned to hug and kiss my wife, and said: "OK, I got to go."

I had been driving around the city until 11 p.m., then I had met my wife at the club where she was celebrating with friends. Now I was about to head back on the road. It was one of the most money-making nights of the year.

I got in my car and turned on the application. I got a request a few blocks east of where I was and drove to pick up my fare.

"So where are you going?" I asked the passenger as he got in.

"I'm going to Rosemont."

"Oh no!" I said, before I could stop myself.

"Is there a problem?"

"Well, I was hoping that you were heading downtown. That's where I can make the most money tonight."

"Do you want me to cancel the ride?" he asked, annoyed.

"Not at all. I will take you where you want to go. Happy new year!" I added with a smile. But inside I was screaming: I don't want to go all the way to Rosemont! That's so far away from downtown.

Luckily the roads were almost empty. I got out there in record time.

But as soon as that man got out, I got another request from a casino nearby.

I drove to the casino, but before the passenger got in my car I let him know: "I am driving back to downtown and am only going to pick you up if you are heading that way."

"Yeah, that's where I'm going," he said.

The man got in the car and I started telling how glad I was that he was going downtown. "This is the best night of the year, I can make a lot of money with the surge prices."

I jumped on the expressway and was at Division and State in only a few minutes.

"Can you wait for me a minute?" the man said as he got out. "I'm going to get a friend."

Five minutes later, I called him to let him know I was leaving. "I'm coming right back," he said. "Wait for me."

A few minutes later, he knocked on my window. Alone.

"Where is your friend?" I asked.

"He didn't want to come. Just take me back."

"Take you back where? Your friend's house?"

"No. Take me back to the casino," he said.

I couldn't believe it. I had wasted a lot of time waiting for him, and now I had to go back to the suburbs. "No problem," I said without smiling. In my head I was calling him all sort of names. But I started driving.

"I will get you a big tip," the man said. "I know you wanted to make money, but I needed to get this for my party." He showed me a small plastic bag full of cocaine.

"Put that away!" I screamed as I drove.

"I need to get a hit first," he said. He put his cellphone on his lap and made a line on it. Then he snorted it, right there in my car.

"Put that away!"

"Just one more." He started to make another line.

Just then, I saw a police car. It had pulled over a vehicle just a few blocks ahead. "The cops are right ahead!" I screamed as we got closer. "Put that shit away!"

"Relax," he said. "The cops don't mind."

I was only half a block away and the man was still snorting cocaine.

Finally, just as we passed the cops, the man put the bag away and waved to them. "See, I told you there was no problem," he smiled at me.

I drove as fast as I could, so I could get to the casino and get rid of him.

"Happy New Year!" the man said when he got out. "I'll give you a big tip!"

I drove away without saying anything.

A few minutes later my phone announced that I had gotten a tip. I looked at my phone to see it.

Five dollars.

I pulled over the side of the road and turned off my phone. It was too late to try to head downtown. And I was too upset to drive. I was upset at the small tip. But mostly I was mad because I knew that if I had been pulled over by the cops, they would have seen the cocaine, and the man would have blamed it on me. And who were the cops going to believe? A white man from suburbia, or an immigrant from Guatemala driving a car for a ride sharing company on New Year's?

A few days later, I was getting ready to start another night of driving. I took a shower, got dressed, and went to my dresser to put on socks, only to find I had no clean socks.

"What happened to my socks?" I asked my wife, knowing already that she had borrowed several of my socks during the week.

That started an argument about the different things that she asks me to do around the house, like not to leave my shoes in the middle of the floor, and to wash the dishes more often. And all the kind of things I wish she did more often…

Finally I fished the socks I had just taken off out of the laundry basket. "I don't have time to argue," I told my wife as I left the house.

I drove around the city for a couple of hours, and then I got a request to pick up a lady. I drove to the address, and as I got there, a man got in.

He sat in the passenger seat. "My wife ordered the ride," he said. "She'll be here soon."

He gave me the address to the restaurant they were going to.

We sat and waited. A few minutes later, he made a phone call. "What is taking you so long? I'm already in the car!"

We waited some more. Five minutes later, he made another call. "Are we still going out? Or should I get back in the house?"

Five minutes later, his wife got in the car. "Why do you have to rush me all the time?" she asked angrily.

"Why did you order the car if you weren't ready?" he answered, a little too loud. "It isn't fair to make the driver wait so long for you to get out of the house."

I thought: oh no, don't get me involved in this.

"He doesn't mind waiting," the lady replied.

I started driving. I thought: I got out of my house so I wouldn't have to deal with this kind of thing.

"Wait!" the lady suddenly said. "You're going the wrong way!"

"He knows where he's going," the husband said. "I gave him the address to the restaurant."

"But we have to pick up…" She said a name I can't remember.

"I hate them," the husband replied. "If I knew they were coming, I'd have stayed at home."

"What do you expect?" she said. "If we go out by ourselves, we'll be arguing all the time."

"No, we won't!" he said.

By then I was giving the guy some serious side eye. I couldn't help myself.

I got to the address the lady gave me, and there was a couple outside kissing. They stopped when they saw the car.

"After you, dear," the man said, holding the door open for her.

They said hello to the couple already in the car, and they started kissing again. I had to tell them to stop kissing and put on their seatbelts so I could start driving. The drive to the restaurant was a short one, but they kept holding hands the whole way there.

The man got out of the car, and again held the door open for his wife. The guy in the passenger seat, his wife, and I all rolled our eyes at the same time.

Then the man in the passenger seat got out, ran over to the side of the car where his wife was sitting, and held the door open for her. "After you, dear," he said, making fun of the other guy. The husband and wife started to laugh as they made their way inside.

A few days later, my wife and I again got in an argument about me leaving my shoes in the middle of the floor.

The next morning before my wife woke up, I got ready for work, and I arranged a surprise for her.

She sent me a text later that day: "very funny I love you too." She sent a picture of the message I had left for her. I had put my shoes in the middle of the floor, forming a heart and a letter U.

The following night I went out on the road again, and again I drove close to twelve hours straight.

It was five minutes to 4:00 a.m. when I received a final request. I drove to pick up my passenger, hoping they were going toward my house. But they were going to Naperville. It was good to get a long ride, but I knew I would end up far from home, and I knew I would have to ride back with no passenger.

I must have looked just as tired as I was feeling, because the passengers asked me if I wanted them to cancel the ride. I almost took their offer, but I figured one more right wouldn't hurt.

There are several questions that passengers ask their drivers in order to start a conversation. Like: Where are you from? (Probably due to my heavy Latino accent I got asked that one the most, followed by: How long you been driving?) However, that night my passengers asked a question I had not heard before: "What made you decide to work for a ridesharing company?"

The obvious answer would have been: To make some extra money. But I found myself telling them about how one day I had seen a car with a mustache driving by, and then found myself months later with a mustache attached to my own vehicle.

They didn't ask any more questions, but as they sat silently in the back seat, my mind went back in time to a time years before I saw the car with the mustache.

I was unemployed and looking for work in the help-wanted ads in the local paper.

TAXI DRIVERS NEEDED had caught my eye, and I had called the company from the ad. They gave me several options: I could use my own vehicle, but it needed to pass an inspection and would probably require some upgrades. I could lease a vehicle from them, but the money for the monthly lease would be deducted from the earnings. Or, for hundreds of thousands of dollars, I could buy a car and a medallion from them.

As an unemployed person in desperate need of income, that last option had seemed the most ridiculous to me. In the end, I had found a job serving tables in a restaurant and the whole idea of driving a taxi had been forgotten.

But as I drove, I wondered how differently it would had been if I had taken the choice of leasing a car and driving a taxi, compared to the ridesharing work I was now doing.

The first thing that occurred to me was the fact that taxi drivers often got robbed, whereas ridesharing drivers didn't exchange any money with their passengers, as long as everything went through the app.

Second, although my car had to pass an inspection, it didn't need any upgrades besides the mustache on the front.

And finally, there was no need to invest in an expensive medallion. In fact, I had been given a bonus every time I signed up for a company. Putting gas into my car late at night, I had heard from more than one taxi driver how they had spent decades saving to buy a medallion and be their own boss, only to have their investment lose its value with the introduction of the ridesharing technology.

I was bothered by that. But also glad that I had dodged that bullet.

After all, I had wanted to drive a taxi, and I had wanted to make some extra money. Things were getting serious between me and my girlfriend. But I had some major credit card debt that I wanted to pay off before I could make any major commitments. I felt that with two previous marriages, I was already bringing enough baggage to our relationship, without adding financial baggage to it.

And working for the ridesharing companies had helped. In fact, I had almost put in order my finances. I was even starting to have some savings. Soon I could give up one of my jobs. It was just a matter of choosing between my job in the morning at the factory, or my night job driving around.

After I dropped off my passenger, I started to head back to Chicago, but I stopped at a gas station. When I tried to get out to pump the gas, I felt a sharp pain in my lower back. I was barely able to stand for the few minutes it took to fill the car up. It was difficult to drive back home, and it was even more difficult to get out of bed the next morning.

All those long nights of driving had finally caught up with me. That's the main reason why I don't drive for a ridesharing company anymore. That, and the fact that it just doesn't pay as much as it used to.

But if I have to be honest, I must admit that I miss it. I miss seeing all the parts of the city, but I miss having conversations the most, even those conversations with people I didn't agree with. I miss listening to other people's life stories, and telling them a little bit about mine. I miss having the opportunity to get out of my bubble and meet other people with other ideas. I think that it is important that we all find ways to get out of our bubbles.

Especially now, now that it's so hard to do so.

As a nation we are taking a ride into the unknown. It's a ride that will probably be more of a rollercoaster than anything else. Perhaps more, uncertain, dangerous or scary than we had imagined. It's a ride that might not be safe for all of us, but it's a ride that we must try and survive together.

Acknowledgments

First and foremost, I would like to thank my parents. (As I write this sentence I can hear my mom's voice: "Tu papa no hizo nada, yo te crie solita"—your dad didn't do anything, I raised you all by myself. Which is mostly true since my mom was always the bread winner, but I still have to thank him too, Mom.)

To my siblings (all six of them) for the few and many memories bad and good, mostly good, that we share together and for putting up with me during my worst times.

To all my friends and teachers from school who were the first to read some of my early writings.

To Threadless for giving me a chance with their Type Tees (submit a slogan) contest. It gave me an opportunity at writing my first very short stories. To the Threadless community, the friends I made and the sloganeers that nurtured my imagination, the illustrators that made my ideas into t-shirt designs; and especially thanks to Victor Callahan for helping in the cover design of this book, and to

JoAnn Koh, who for years has encouraged me to write more stories.

To sweet Mel, Melissa Pavlik my wife, my love, my friend; for encouraging me to share my stories and having faith on me. Without you, I doubt that I had ever tried my hand at live storytelling. Thank you for being so patient with me. I know I can be a handful. (I can picture my ex-wives nodding in agreement as I typed those words.)

So many thanks to all the storytellers, the ones whose stories I read, heard in songs or poems, or watched on screen or in person as I was growing up. Thanks for planting the seed.

To Rick Kogan, who read one of my first stories and encouraged me to keep writing.

To Luis Tubens, whose poetry and stage presence inspired me and continues to inspire me.

To Shannon Cason for making a path for many people like myself here in Chicago.

To Archy Arch one of the first and best storytellers I have ever heard. (Amazingly AA has proven to be as amazing as a friend as he is at storytelling.)

To Lily Be, whose "Doñas of Humboldt Park" story blasted thru the radio waves at a time when I had convinced myself that no one would be interested to hear the kind of stories I had to tell.

To Scott Whitehair, your storytelling class gave me the confidence to keep sharing but also introduce me to my dear classmates and friends.

To GPA, from whom I have learned so much since the first time I heard him tell a story.

To the Moth, and all those working to make the Moth slams and other shows a reality. To every storytelling show producer that has invited me to perform on their show, and all the storytellers I have met at those events, I want to thank each of you by name but I can hear my editor telling me I only have one page. (I think I already took two, and I still have many people to thank.)

Del Dominguez and Laura Florez of Mixed Motion Art Dance Academy for letting me practice my first story at one of their Mambo socials.

All the storytellers that have share a story at our "80 Minutes Around the World" immigration storytelling show, and Angel Ling, who helped turn the show into a podcast. She is like a real angel.

To Erin Barker (a remarkable storyteller whose stories I have watched dozens of times). She helped find our New York show a home at Caveat.

To all my friends for your support on our live and virtual shows.

To Matthew Dicks, your incredible achievements on the Moth stage opened my eyes to the kind of things I could do.

To everyone that was kind enough to write a blurb for this book I will be forever grateful.

To my editor and publisher. God knows I was not an easy person to work with, too many ideas, too many questions, just too much.

To my kids, Miriam and Geovanni. I wish that someday I can make you feel a tenth as proud as you have made feel from the very moment I knew of your existence.

And to you, who are about to read this book: eternamente agradecido.

— Nestor "The Boss" Gomez

About the Author

Nestor "The Boss" Gomez was born in Guatemala and moved to Chicago undocumented in the mid-80s. He has won over forty Moth Slams and is a three-time Chicago Moth Grand Slam winner. He is also the creator, producer, curator and host of "80 Minutes Around the World," a storytelling show that features the stories of immigrants, their descendants, and allies.

About Tortoise Books

Slow and steady wins in the end, even in publishing. Tortoise Books is dedicated to finding and promoting quality authors who haven't yet found a niche in the marketplace—writers producing memorable and engaging works that will stand the test of time.

Learn more at www.tortoisebooks.com, find us on Facebook, or follow us on Twitter @TortoiseBooks.

CPSIA information can be obtained
at www.ICGtesting.com
Printed in the USA
LVHW021345070721
692095LV00004B/311